# Teaching and Learning the New Economics

# Members of the Economics 16–19 Project:

*National Coordinator*
**Linda Thomas**

*Steering Group*
**Richard Layard**
Jim Bennett
Diane Billam
Bill Callaghan
Jim Clifford
Jack Cobbe
Sami Daniel
Ian Dorton
David Greenaway
Alan Hamlin
Kay Kellaway
Noel Kershaw
Frank Livesey
Delyth Robinson
Keith Robinson
Angus Taylor
Philip Warland
Roy Wilkinson

*London RDG*
**Paul Clarke**
Richard Baty
Mike Douglass
Roy Ecclestone
Paul Egan
Colin Harber-Stuart
David Jones
Steve Lepper
Caroline Loewenstein
Adrian Lyons
Dean Lythgoe
Tom Smith
John Troy
Steve Williams

*Midlands RDG*
**Brian Hill**
**Tim Maxfield**
Alain Anderton
Ian Birth
Chris Evans
Martin Frayn
Andrew Hale
Barry Harrison
Lester Hunt
David Lewis
Tim Mason
Maggie Matthews
Peter Newton-Lewis
Jacqui Smith
Jill Smith
David Swainston
Graham Teager
Mike Tighe
Simon Whitehouse
Richard Wootton

*Northern RDG*
**Clive Riches**
Andrew Aberdeen
Jeremy Abrahams
Philip Armstrong
John Ashworth
Mark Bushnall
Felicity Furlong
Andrew Gouge
Christine Lawson
Gary Lovelace
Howard McWilliam
Stephen Robson
Dominic Speed
Peter Thomas
Jeremy Williams

*Northwest RDG*
**Linda Hall**
David Badley
Roy Bradburn
Paul Canning
Ian Chambers
Joan Davies
Richard Dunnill
Steve Foster
Steve Gentry
Simon Gill
David Hall
Morag Kennedy
Jean Long
Jeff Marsh
Kevin Mattinson
Jim Nettleship
Sue Robson
John Shanahan
Bill Tomlinson
Peter Townley

*Southern RDG*
**Geoff Hale**
Steve Brown
Pat Cooper
Robert Cooper
Kate Hallett
Mac McConnel
Julia Mortimer
Rob Thomas

*Southwest RDG*
**Dave Dickson**
**John Ryan**
Jack Cobbe
Richard Haupt
Lin Phelps
Dianne Small
Linda Williams

*Content NDG*
**Barry McCormick**
Jeremy Abrahams
Charles Bean
John Beath
Paul Clarke
Tony Cockerill
Tony Culyer
Adrian Darnell
Charles Feinstein
Bernie Gillman
Steve Hodkinson
Linda Thomas

*Teaching & Learning NDG*
**Chris Vidler**
Ken Cole
Deidre Eastburn
Alma Harris
Chris Leonard
Linda Thomas

*Teacher Development NDG*
**Steve Hodkinson**
Paul Clarke
Dave Dickson
Geoff Hale
Linda Hall
Brian Hill
Tim Maxfield
Clive Riches
John Ryan

*Editorial*
Christopher Dent
Steve Hodkinson
Frank Livesey
Linda Thomas
Chris Vidler
Sue Walton
Robert Wilson
Keith Wood

*Executive Committee*
**Linda Thomas**
Brian Atkinson
Steve Hodkinson
Wendy Sterling
Allan Stewart
Chris Vidler
Sue Walton
Phil Ward
Richard Young

RDG = Regional Development Group
NDG = National Development Group
The names printed in **bold** type are chairpersons of groups.

**THE ECONOMICS 16-19 PROJECT**

# Teaching and Learning the New Economics

Barry McCormick
AND
Chris Vidler

*Edited by Linda Thomas*

Heinemann

Heinemann Educational
A division of Heinemann Publishers (Oxford) Ltd
Halley Court, Jordan Hill, Oxford OX2 8EJ

OXFORD LONDON EDINBURGH
MADRID ATHENS BOLOGNA PARIS
MELBOURNE SYDNEY AUCKLAND
SINGAPORE TOKYO IBADAN NAIROBI
HARARE GABORONE PORTSMOUTH NH (USA)

© Economics & Business Education Association 1994

First published 1994

98 97 96 95 94
10 9 8 7 6 5 4 3 2 1

**A catalogue record for this book is available from the British Library**

ISBN 0 435 33100 0

Designed by Pentacor PLC, High Wycombe, Bucks

Printed and bound in Great Britain by Clays Ltd, St Ives plc

# Contents

**INTRODUCTION**

| | |
|---|---|
| The Economics 16–19 Project | 1 |
| Content and the new economics | 3 |
| Teaching and learning the new economics | 4 |
| Curriculum development | 5 |

**PART 1:** Content and the new economics

| | |
|---|---|
| What should be taught to economics students at 16–19? | 7 |
| Justifying the choice of concepts to teach | 10 |
| Aspirations for A and A/S level economics and Advanced GNVQs | 10 |
| The organizing principle | 15 |
| Core content | 15 |
|     *Building blocks* | 16 |
|     *'Alternative approaches' to mainstream economics* | 18 |
| Compulsory content | 18 |
|     *Macroeconomics* | 19 |
|     *Economic history* | 23 |
|     *Applied data analysis* | 25 |
|     *The economic function of an institution* | 26 |
| Options | 26 |
| Conclusions | 28 |

**PART 2:** Teaching and learning and the new economics

| | |
|---|---|
| Introduction | 29 |
| Current research on learning | 31 |
|     *Classroom thoughtfulness* | 32 |
|     *Students' perceptions of understanding* | 34 |
|     *Learning for meaning* | 35 |

A review of current practice 37
  *Assessment* 37
  *Broadening the learning base through independent investigation* 40
Recommendations 42
  *The student as learner* 43
  *Organizational contexts* 46
  *Relationships* 47
Conclusions 48
References 48

**APPENDICES**

1 Criticisms of academic economics syllabuses at A level 51
2 Microeconomics: further comments on A level 53
3 Essential ingredients of alternative approaches in the A level syllabus 57

# Introduction

## THE ECONOMICS 16–19 PROJECT

In 1991, the then Economics Association formally established the Economics Education 16–19 Project to take economics education into the twenty-first century. The Association's intentions for the project were summarized in its statement of aims, which were:

- to stimulate and co-ordinate a fundamental review of the nature of economics thinking in response to the last decade's shift in the basic concerns of the discipline
- by focusing on the full range of academic and vocational contexts at 16–19, to consider the implications of this review for teaching, learning and assessment strategies
- to develop and publish teaching materials and resources
- to publish the results of the review of the discipline.

Initially, three National and six Regional Development Groups were briefed to undertake specialist research tasks in specific areas. Academic economists were asked for advice on appropriate content at 16–19 in the light of recent developments within economics. Economics educators were asked to advise on the implications of these innovations in the context of teaching and learning. A teacher development group was asked to monitor the training needs of teachers and in this way to facilitate the process of change and development. Economics teachers in schools and colleges were asked 'What do we know about the way students think in economics?' Over two hundred teachers, working within the Regional Development Groups (RDGs), responded to this base-lining question by working systematically with individual students to obtain reliable data about their thoughts in particular areas in economics. The extensive interviewing highlighted a number of obstacles to learning (for example, commonly held misconceptions and preconceptions) and influenced the work of the National Development Groups (NDGs).

The project then moved forward by drawing on its collaborative strengths. Papers and materials were circulated between and within the nine groups. These generated a range of questions for further discussion. Teachers, academic economists and economists working in a range of professional occupations learned from one another and from students. In this way, a common framework was established for the materials development stage of the project, when ideas for classroom resources, based on the project's research, were developed into materials for students and guidance for teachers.

This book documents the work of the NDGs for *Content* and for *Teaching and Learning*, in collaboration with other members of the project. Their work on the nature of economics and its teaching and learning has allowed the project to determine *what* students might learn in economics and *how* they might do so. They argue that:

- **The new economics** assists students to appreciate the power of economics as an important tool to analyse, explain and evaluate the strengths and weaknesses of the market economy in which they live and work, to establish the need for intervention and to assess the appropriateness and impact of different forms of intervention. It requires us to generate learning activities which distinguish between economics and the economic system which is the focus of study.

- **The new economics** expects students to develop their theoretical knowledge, skills and understanding through investigation and analysis of the economic institutions, issues and phenomena with which economists routinely deal. It requires us to abandon the 'theory followed by application' rule which is common in economics texts but which does not reflect the way that economists develop or apply their tools of analysis in practice.

- **The new economics** encourages students to approach the task of learning economics as a whole, to bring the full range of knowledge and expertise which they possess to bear on the exploration of each new context and to recognize the need to develop and expand existing concepts and skills. It requires us to emphasize the inter-relatedness of the discipline's constructs rather than their fragmentation.

- **The new economics** challenges students to become actively and thoughtfully involved in the learning process, to locate new insights in relation to their existing knowledge of the economic system and to respond creatively to the challenges involved in generating new meaning. It requires us to provide opportunities for students to review and reflect on their understanding at every stage in the learning process.

## CONTENT AND THE NEW ECONOMICS

The Economics Content NDG was asked to:

- undertake a fundamental review of the subject
- provide a common brief for all RDGs
- determine the areas of work to be undertaken by the project's RDGs
- allocate specialist areas of work to the appropriate RDGs
- monitor the validity of the economics subject matter contained in materials, resources and guidelines.

Part 1 of this book is an account of the work done to meet the first two objectives.

The group began by seeking teachers' and students' views on the nature of A level economics, and by inviting academic economists to review recent developments within the discipline and its current priorities and, in the light of their review, to advise on appropriate content at 16–19. The reports formed the basis for discussion and reflection by the group during a nine-month period. In May 1992, an interim report was made available to the project for the purpose of initiating further discussion.

In December 1992, the project submitted a report to the then Secondary Examinations and Assessment Council's (SEAC) working group on the A/AS core for economics. It represented the project's views on the nature, form and structure of economics. It recommended that any revised A level course should contain:

- a greater emphasis on the application of basic economic skills
- more economic analysis of, and inference using, simple data sets
- increased analysis of important economic institutions and resource allocation within those institutions
- less allocation of time to issues not directly of interest to a young person taking a single economics course while still laying the foundations for further academic study
- greater preparation for students wishing to undertake individual studies that are a useful preparation for working life
- a greater emphasis on the understanding of public policy issues such as the economic aspects of health, transport, environment, housing, etc.

The report was sufficiently influential to ensure that discussion of the specification of Core Knowledge, Understanding and Skills by the

SEAC working group reflected the project's views and recommendations.

At the same time, the National Council for Vocational Qualifications (NCVQ) was finalizing plans for the introduction of GNVQ. In December 1992, the project was invited to submit two mandatory units for the new Business GNVQ at level 3. The project made recommendations for the performance criteria, range and evidence indicators for three elements within each unit. Once again, the published units were written in accordance with the project's views and recommendations.

Part 1 of this book has been written as the result of a lengthy process of discussion within the project. Because of the project's involvement with the SEAC and NCVQ groups it also incorporates the insights gained there.

## TEACHING AND LEARNING THE NEW ECONOMICS

The Teaching and Learning NDG was asked to:

- produce a research report on economics teaching and learning at 16–19
- undertake a review of the potential of available strategies and resources (e.g. independent learning techniques)
- provide and maintain a common framework for any classroom work undertaken as part of the project
- monitor the classroom effectiveness of materials, resources and guidelines
- build a directory of information and data resources.

Part 2 of this book is an account of the work done by the group to meet the first three objectives. Members attempted to summarize research and discussion undertaken over a nine-month period and to produce a planning framework for use in informing and guiding colleagues working within the project to produce learning materials and strategies.

At the outset, group members felt that much current teaching of economics failed to equip even the most successful students with a conceptual framework which empowered them either in the academic sense (providing access to the discipline's core purpose) or in terms of preparation for everyday life (allowing them to make sense of the economic phenomena and institutions with which they were likely to interact). Furthermore, group members had experience of taking part in various innovations in the teaching of economics, some of which clearly showed that it was possible to organize more active classrooms than those often traditionally associated with economics. However, they were uneasy about whether or not greater activity was always an indication of greater effectiveness and rigour.

They set themselves a number of interrelated tasks. They wished to:

- be clearer in their thinking as to what constitutes learning that is active, effective and rigorous
- use current research on learning to help to deepen and clarify their thinking
- to make a selective review and to evaluate the success of current practice in terms of teaching and learning in economics.

Part 2 is a report of their findings in respect of these tasks and the conclusions and recommendations reached by them. They agreed at the first meeting to translate the proposals for teaching and learning into a set of criteria which could be used to develop materials and approaches to learning. These criteria are also included as Figure 4.

## CURRICULUM DEVELOPMENT

The project was established by the Economics and Business Education Association in response to the need for basic research and development in the area of 16–19 economics. It set itself the task of devising a framework which would deliver an economics education for all 16–19 year old students into the 21st century. The project has deliberately anticipated the institutional changes which are likely to occur during the next ten years (for example, the further modularization of post-16 courses) and incorporated them in its plans. It is against this background, rather than the developments presently taking place in the design of core economics and examination syllabuses, that the project's perspective on the nature and purpose of 16–19 economics should be interpreted. The project's influence on SCAA's 1993 specification of the core of A level economics and on NCVQ's 1993 specification of the Advanced GNVQ in Business has been fundamental. But, since the project has laid the foundation for long-term as well as immediate development, it goes beyond those specifications.

# Part 1
# Content and the new economics

**WHAT SHOULD BE TAUGHT TO ECONOMICS STUDENTS AT 16–19?**

Put simply, our response to this question is: those conceptual frameworks which are helpful in shedding light on some of the major economic problems of our time, and which, in more sophisticated forms, constitute 'what economists do'. Thus the content should be directed at, for example, a thoughtful understanding of why unemployment arises and the role of government in tackling unemployment; or how levels of pollution are determined, why these levels may exceed those which are socially preferred, and how policy may enable a socially preferred outcome to be obtained.

There are a number of basic economic principles or concepts which are more primitive than, and underpin, these problem-orientated conceptual frameworks, but which by themselves provide insufficient structure to explain central economic problems. Examples include opportunity cost, equilibrium, competition, monopoly and externalities. We expect students to become familiar with these basic economic concepts – if possible, more so than in the past – but we believe that economics for 16–19 year old students will be most effectively taught if students are not presented at the heart of the course with a sequence of such concepts supported primarily by brief illustrations. For the simplest abstractions – say opportunity cost or monopoly – this may not pose great intellectual obstacles for 16–19 year olds; but for concepts that involve more complex interrelationships, such as the working of a competitive industry, theory needs to be extensively justified by, and explained within, a sequence of worked applied problems some of which are of transparent interest and central economic importance. For example, students should be introduced to the key implications of the competitive industry model by drawing on data from a selected UK industry. Furthermore, students should be able not only to apply a pre-specified primitive concept, but also to recognize in an everyday context when a particular concept can be adopted.

Greater emphasis ought to be placed on the need for students to come to terms with certain central public policy issues, and on their ability to recognize contexts in which primitive concepts should be adopted to achieve insights. For this to happen, there needs to be a reduction in emphasis elsewhere. We believe this should be done to achieve a significant improvement in the quality of A level education, both academic and vocational. We suggest that the cuts should occur within those 'theoretical' sections of the material which are better left for a higher level course. Two classes of material are expendable:

- theory that is most concerned with laying foundations for advanced study (for example, the foundations of demand theory)
- those areas of theory (for example, oligopoly) where advanced models are presented as better representations of reality but in most cases are learned only mechanically and not in a form which lends itself to selective applications in a variety of contexts.

We would prefer a situation where young people can readily and selectively apply basic price theory to one where they can only sketchily and mechanically reproduce a wider range of models.

Most of the preceding comments apply primarily to microeconomics, which in modern texts is fundamental to *all* branches of economics and is not, as it has sometimes been taught, separate from and intellectually in parallel with macroeconomics. This is reflected in our proposed structure for a course in economics. Fortunately the principles upon which economists now draw to study microeconomic policy in areas of health, transport, environmental issues etc. are identical in modern mainstream thinking to the principles they use to study and justify policy choice in the areas of macroeconomics (unemployment, inflation, balance of payments, growth etc.). The same is also true in the area of international trade. A major theme in our discussions has been how to encourage the teaching of macroeconomics as an extension of core micro-thinking and to dispose of various arbitrary constructs that block ready access to this branch of the discipline. We also believe that 'essential' Keynesianism, amongst other macro schools, should not be associated with certain diagrams incapable of contrasting paradigms. It should rather be associated with assumptions about behaviour and with the diagrams that illustrate the consequences of these and other assumptions. In this way students can most directly be introduced to differences in modern macro-thinking, and move fluently between alternative approaches.

If A level courses, both academic and vocational, are to place a more direct emphasis on 'training for life' and provide a preparation for further degree studies while retaining substantial intellectual rigour, what does this imply?

• There needs to be a greater emphasis on the frameworks required to achieve an understanding of the more accessible public policy issues, such as economic aspects of environment, health, education, housing, privatization – issues that are likely to remain at the centre of political debate, and which are also important aspects of vocational courses. These frameworks are also suitable for the provision of appropriate concepts to guide project work towards more analytical and less descriptive investigations. In their more advanced form, they provide the challenging, coherent, logical constructions that discipline the economic approach and make it exciting for young people.

• There needs to be a greater recognition that an economy can be viewed as a *system* of interrelated markets, which under *certain strong assumptions* will allocate resources efficiently as in Adam Smith's Invisible Hand theorem. By stressing the 'system' of interrelated markets, students will study problems relating changes in market 1 to outcomes in market 2. With a greater awareness of two key market distortions – monopolies and externalities – they will be able to recognize how to use elementary concepts to understand policy intervention.

• There needs to be a greater emphasis on the understanding and intuitive application of basic economic skills, rather than merely a mechanical demonstration of a wider range of models and points of theory.

• There should be a greater awareness of the economic determinants and functions of certain institutions such as trade unions, the family, or a building society, where we distinguish the economic structure and role of the organization from a simplistic description of its frequency, size or tasks.

• There should be a greater emphasis on *long-run* issues in macro-economics (e.g. growth and trade) rather than the present focus on short-run cyclical considerations.

• There needs to be a greater emphasis on the ability to select data and economic argument in order to answer questions appertaining to a recent period of monetary and fiscal policy.

Finally, by way of introduction, we should stress that we believe that the acquisition of *simple* mathematical and statistical techniques, their various applications in the analysis of data sets, and the study of fairly elementary economic problems using such analysis, is both important and deserving of further development. This is one of the ways in which A level economics provides a basis for developing transferable and extremely useful post-education skills.

## JUSTIFYING THE CHOICE OF CONCEPTS TO TEACH

Firstly, for about 80 per cent of students, A level is the final or highest level of economics instruction. Thus there is an overwhelming argument for the view that A level should be a course suited to the perceived needs – both intellectual and practical – of those for whom A level will be the only formal educational preparation for the economic aspects of their lives as citizens and members of the labour force. A course directed at current controversies and the use of basic economic principles seems best suited to the needs of the majority of students.

Secondly, it seems reasonable to suggest that it will be in the interests of society as a whole to ensure that those leaving A level courses can understand some of the most basic principles that economists adopt when advising on the major issues of the day. In this way the electorate is more likely to understand the preferred economic strategy, and governments more able to act without the constraint of ignorance of economic knowledge. Thus teaching a policy-based course is appropriate to the needs of the country as a whole, as well as to those of the students concerned.

Thirdly, a course based on 'economic problems' is more likely to attract student interest than one based on economic principles.

## ASPIRATIONS FOR A AND A/S LEVEL ECONOMICS AND ADVANCED GNVQs

It will be helpful to summarize the breadth of economics before we proceed to state our aspirations for students. Economics is the study of how choices, framed by the scarcity of resources, explain the extent and character of material well-being, together with the nature of the institutional and social fabric. Thus economic analysis encompasses not only familiar issues such as the creation and distribution of wealth, but also broader issues reflecting the structure of society – to include matters as diverse as certain aspects of the behaviour of the family, whether there should be a state pension scheme or merely private schemes, and the extent to which government choices over expenditure and taxation should be allocated to local or national levels, and whether tolls should be levied on major roads. Our preference is that students should gain a greater understanding of the use of the most seminal economic ideas in a broad range of contexts, and in particular how a quite small number of concepts can be used to understand behaviour in many different applied areas. This we believe will require more focus on a few principles than has perhaps been commonplace.

These principles are understood and made operative through *extensive practice*. Indeed without *much* practice, it does not seem to us to be remotely possible that students will be able, for example, to recognize a context in which a clear case for policy intervention can be constructed, or be able to discuss intelligently the implications of a change in one market for a number of related markets. We suspect that some of the present concern with A level microeconomics content may reflect its fragmented structure and thus a tendency for it to be viewed as a sequence of unrelated micro-models, with little insight offered for the market economy and its properties. This theme is further developed in Appendix 1 and Appendix 2, which outline the major criticisms of the kinds of A and A/S level syllabuses that have dominated the teaching of academic economics in the past, and which also examine the nature of microeconomics.

If we are to constrain the range of applied skills required of our students, then we need to *limit* the range of economic models that they will need to learn and deploy. But which models should these be? We should presumably teach a range of connected and, in the main, reinforcing frameworks which explain resource allocation in the world today. Inevitably these will be the simplest models that provide the key ideas that we wish to convey at this level. For the foreseeable future the relevant economic context is the 'market economy' and, given the development of modern society throughout the developed and partially developed world, it is sensible that this central fact should be reflected in the curriculum. It is worth pausing to stress that the expression 'market economy' is a broad one which refers to a range of economies, all of which experience substantial government involvement, despite the overriding characteristic that the bulk of resources is allocated by trade between private sector firms and individuals. Thus the 'market economy' we have in mind is the predominant political/economic model in western economies.

The ambiguities in defining the 'market economy' immediately suggest a range of issues about which we expect our students to have some understanding – the notions of markets, trade and output in such an economy; the nature and consequence of government involvement;

and both the structural and cyclical characteristics of the economy. We may justify this direction in terms of:

- enabling young people to understand the economic underpinning to current political debate and the rationales for and against market economies
- enabling young people to understand the common economic ideas and principles which can be applied in both micro (individual market) and macro (economy-wide) contexts, rather than seeing these areas as separate subjects
- giving young people direct access to lively debate in the micro policy areas of housing, health etc. that include such issues as how 'output' and 'efficiency' are measured, and the role of government
- giving young people as clear an historical perspective as time allows into the evolution of certain market outcomes and the changing role of government policy in these markets.

Thus economics at 16–19 should inform students of how the participants and institutions of a market economy make choices and how these choices are interrelated. It should also inform young people how economists perceive the role of government in a market economy so that they have a more informed and insightful view of the economic climate in which they live as citizens and vote as members of the electorate. This analysis should culminate in succinct insights into the strengths and weaknesses of the market economy, including empirical and theoretical insight into why certain economies have been more successful than others in generating material well-being and protecting the disadvantaged.

As a result, young people in their working lives can become more effective in making resource allocation decisions, with more understanding of the allocative problems faced by other individuals within various institutions. They can also be more capable of investing wisely in the accumulation of human skills throughout their lives.

Within this framework we think it is reasonable that A level economists, whether engaged in academic or vocational studies, should have access to and be able to use certain applied skills. These are outlined in Figure 1.

Economics students at 16–19 need to work in applied settings so as to be able to do the following:
- Explain how individuals gain from trade with other individuals in goods and services.
- Explain what is meant by economic efficiency for an economy as a whole.
- Use provided data to construct and interpret a production possibility frontier for a simple economy.
- Relate this to the behaviour of a competitive economy which satisfies certain assumptions.
- Show what is meant by an efficient allocation of resources within the specific organizational context of a firm and a non-market institution, such as a school, prison or hospital.
- Explain how a single shock to a market economy – for example, the collapse of demand for coal – leads to a series of repercussions, and to predict (i) in which markets repercussions would be large or small, and (ii) where the greatest mobility of inputs would be required.
- Show how the resources used by an industry are changed if (i) the cost structure of producing the industry's output changes, (ii) the demand for the product changes, (iii) the product is supplied by a monopolist, and (iv) an input becomes more scarce.
- Show how an entrepreneur making a business investment, or a decision to enter a market, is influenced by both the microeconomic circumstances faced by the individual firm and the various monetary and fiscal instruments which determine the macroeconomic environment.
- Show how government policy may raise economic efficiency in certain specific contexts: namely, where there exist monopolies, externalities or public goods.
- Identify the presence of monopolies, externalities and public goods in different market contexts (for example, housing, education, health) and thus operationalize understanding of the circumstances in which economists regard that governments should and should not intervene in a market economy.
- Analyse the implications – in the short and long run – of prices being fixed at levels different from market clearing prices.

- Analyse the implications, for unemployment levels and inflation, of wages set above market clearing levels.
- Analyse the broad factors which may have influenced the success of firms in certain economies relative to those elsewhere.
- Explain how the nature of the firm has changed in the twentieth century, and why firms in certain economies have prospered while those elsewhere have been less successful.
- Explain the distribution of earnings and total income between different types of household, and be able to relate this to educational achievement and worker experience (and be able to analyse whether economic discrimination is arising in a workplace).
- Explain the objectives of negotiators representing firms and trade unions and show the likely consequences of their behaviour for the decisions of the firm.
- Explain the overall budgetary problem faced by a Chancellor of the Exchequer seeking to meet the demands for various expenditures and also the objections to taxation and higher levels of government borrowing.
- Analyse (i) recent monetary and fiscal policy, (ii) the recent two decades of a central microeconomic feature of the economy (e.g. the changing market for higher education or that for housing).
- Carry out simple interpretative exercises using data.
- Distinguish arguments to support a proposition and be able to recognize that correlation and causality differ.
- Use statements involving probability.
- Qualify their conclusions as necessary by language such as 'probably' and 'on the basis of this data' and be able to set out their results and interpretations in a full and meaningful way to include a clear statement of the assumptions upon which their analysis is based.

**Figure 1**  Applied skills

# CONTENT AND THE NEW ECONOMICS

## THE ORGANIZING PRINCIPLE

*The 16–19 curriculum in economics should be organized around the central ideas that both explain the behaviour of the market economy and account for its strengths and weaknesses.*

In examining the behaviour of the market economy it is necessary to study both the economy as a whole and also the various differentiated component parts. We wish to stress that students should study the component parts of the economic system not only with a view to the determinants of the behaviour of each, but also with regard to the *interactions* between the circumstances in related markets. It is a serious deficiency in an economics course to study macroeconomics – aggregate fluctuations, unemployment growth and inflation – on the one hand, and behaviour within individual markets on the other, whilst neglecting the interaction between individual markets. This is unlikely to generate an understanding of the allocation of resources between sectors of the economy. This neglect will leave students unable to analyse how an exogenous change in world prices, tastes, technology, government policy, etc. can alter the *pattern* of production, and final demands, and the allocation of industrial inputs. Since many of our students are likely to become commercial managers, anticipating the implications for expansion or contraction in their sector, and also since many important problems concern changes in the *pattern* of resource allocation, such issues need to be integral to the subject matter, and we return to this below.

It is not our intention to devise a syllabus but instead to provide a somewhat broader framework within which syllabuses with various emphases might be developed. We consider that a structure with three distinctions will be of assistance to most groups responsible for syllabuses in economics. The distinctions we suggest are (i) core content; (ii) compulsory content; (iii) optional content.

## CORE CONTENT

For the core content we have in mind the basic concepts of microeconomics, such as opportunity cost, gains from exchange between individuals, the production possibility frontier, analysis of competitive and monopolistic markets, the Invisible Hand proposition, externalities, public goods. These concepts underpin the theory of resource allocation and policy intervention in a market economy, and a clear understanding of these issues is a requirement before proceeding to study all areas of economics.

## Building blocks

If students are to acquire a working knowledge of the strengths and weaknesses of the market economy, they will need to understand the basic building blocks used by economists to characterize and assess such an economy. The foundation building block is made up of a clear understanding of:

- how a competitive market functions: how supply by individual competitive firms is determined, how this can then be aggregated across firms to determine industry level supply, how entry and exit of firms will occur in response to price fluctuations and thereby influence supply elasticity in the short and long runs
- how the long-run industry supply curve is none other than the long-run industry marginal cost curve, so that in this form of market structure, the price which clears the market will also cause resources to be drawn into the industry to the point where the marginal opportunity cost is just equal to the valuation placed by the purchaser on the marginal unit of output produced
- how to construct the industry demand curve.

It is important to be clear about why students learn the competitive model. The reason is partly to provide basic price theory which can explain outcomes in a variety of contexts. But it is also to gain insight into the basic Invisible Hand theorem which underpins much polemical economic debate and *almost all of what economists recommend* to governments: *under certain assumptions a system of competitive markets will allocate resources in a Pareto-efficient manner.* This result leads economists to prescribe economic policies in most areas of application that rest on being able to identify a market distortion, and then introduce a policy which causes the 'market' to behave as if there were no distortion. Thus students should learn that the proper regulation of the price of a monopolist can cause it to supply output as if it were a competitive industry.

Smith's Invisible Hand requires strong assumptions to achieve this result. But the basic proposition, when coupled with the requisite assumptions, provides a coherent menu of basic building blocks in a student's education, leading to an understanding of how policy intervention should be formulated.

We do not believe that students are prepared at 16–19 for a *full* discussion of the assumptions required for Smith's Invisible Hand result to hold. However, two crucial departures from these assumptions –

externalities and monopolistic markets – make a powerful combination of distortion that explain much policy intervention. Thus students should learn about the implications of monopoly industries and externalities upon resource allocation; the need for 'public good' provision; and, in less analytical detail, the failure of certain prices to adjust to clear markets; the problems which imperfect information can bring. These categories of 'distortions' – so called since they 'distort' the allocation of resources away from those which are Pareto-efficient – generate the leading arguments upon which governments are persuaded by economists to intervene in the market economy, in order to secure a 'Pareto-preferred' outcome and improve welfare. In a variety of contexts students need to develop their understanding of the primitive concepts of externalities and monopoly power and be able to recognize them when presented with practical situations in which to use their economic skills.

For 16–19 year old students it would be preferable to limit the range of market structures to just three types, so that in viewing the economy as a system of (potential) markets, the students would view some as competitive, some as monopolistic, some as 'non-existent' (for example, atmospheric pollution). In the event of distortions in each type of market, the government will adopt regulations, taxes, subsidies and quotas, to influence individual firms and households to use resources as if they were in an undistorted competitive market. By reviewing government policy in a range of markets, students will gain an understanding of the approach that economists take to a broad range of economic policy issues.

It is desirable that students learn that *regulation* (for example, in the context of monopolies) and *taxation* (in the case of negative externality creating outputs) have in common that they are two of the various policies used by governments to correct the misallocation of resources.

Students should become familiar with the concept of Pareto efficiency by using both the concepts of a production possibility frontier and a utility possibility frontier. They could be shown how a Pareto-efficient solution may carry obnoxious distributional implications but that certain instruments – for example, income taxation, social welfare policies etc. – are the primary instruments used to achieve distributional objectives. The selection of most other policy measures is then free to occur at levels which primarily achieve efficiency rather than distributional objectives. Since the major distributional policy instruments have allocational consequences it is almost inevitable that modern economies will operate inside the 'production' and 'utility' possibility frontiers – sacrificing efficiency for distributional objectives.

### 'Alternative approaches' to mainstream economics

The group debated at some length the case for introducing a range of political economy approaches (including Marxist and post-Keynesian) into the core. By a large majority it was decided that such material did not belong in the core for the following reasons.

- The core is deliberately very slight in volume, amounting to only the key concepts universally used by economists.
- To include such material would appear an exception to our decision to choose material that relates to the understanding of clearly established economic problems and is basic to 'what economists do', since only a small percentage of economists follow 'alternative approaches'.

We would not be opposed to such material being introduced in the options, where most examination of social and economic problems will occur, provided the alternative approaches offer testable ideas that might improve upon or partially assist more commonplace theories. If alternative approaches have a role at A level then they must address problems of concern to students in a way which is both scientific and readily intelligible to young people at an early stage of their career.

The group also considered the question of whether 'alternative approaches' might be recommended as an option area. A large majority thought it should not, but this reflected the conflation of two separate arguments. Many thought that an 'alternative approaches' option would prove too obscure and confusing for 16–19 year old students who were more likely to be primarily interested in tackling social economic issues as presented on the news programmes. The member who supported 'alternative approaches' in the core opposed it as an option on the grounds that it either belongs in the core – influencing the whole course structure – or not in the course at all. Another member thought that it could comprise an option, but did not belong in the core.

An invited paper from Dr G. Harcourt suggesting what material any 'alternative approaches' section of an A level course might contain is included as Appendix 3.

### COMPULSORY CONTENT

The compulsory sections of the curriculum contain material which is sufficiently important that students who are studying economics as a substantial element of their course should be required to develop an understanding of it, although the material is not regarded as the underpinning of all economic analysis. The four chief components of this section are (i) macroeconomics, (ii) an economic history element, (iii) applied data analysis, and (iv) the economic function of at least one major institution (e.g. a trade union, the family, building society or firm).

## Macroeconomics

*All students should have an understanding of the aggregate economy. This will require them to draw upon notions of markets and demand and supply developed in the micro course to construct the basic model of aggregate output, inflation and unemployment in a steady state. This will provide a suitable framework for developing an understanding of cycles in aggregate output and the potential for government stabilization policy to smooth these fluctuations. Finally, students should be given insight into the analysis of economic growth, which has been given too little emphasis in comparison with stabilization problems.*

The content of 'core' microeconomics was centred on the idea of developing a few key concepts that underpin the analysis of market economies (in particular the role of prices in allocating resources efficiently), and the limitations to that analysis. It is natural therefore to presuppose that macroeconomics should be organized along similar lines. However, except for the fact that in macroeconomic problems everything usually affects everything else (i.e. that a general rather than partial analysis is required), there is no similar set of core concepts for macroeconomics. Rather it is frequently simply an application of the core microeconomic ideas to macroeconomic questions such as: why is there unemployment? how does inflation come about? why do growth rates and standards of living differ so much between countries?

Introductory presentations of macroeconomics usually start with the circular flow of income, the multiplier process and the determination of national income with the aid of the 45-degree diagram that plots demand $\{C(Y)+I+G\}$ against income (Y).

An analysis of the determination of aggregate demand may be very detailed – introducing ideas such as the investment accelerator and even the interconnection between product and money markets (IS/LM). However, supply considerations are frequently introduced only at a rather late stage, and then usually in an indirect fashion in the shape of the Phillips curve. This has the effect of obscuring the affinity between microeconomic and macroeconomic analysis; indeed they can often seem like alien disciplines to a new student. It also has the effect of obscuring the reasons why macroeconomists so often disagree, because these disagreements are invariably rooted in questions of market failure.

We therefore see macroeconomics best taught not as a separate entity with its own core concepts, which can be applied in various optional modules, but rather as a set of topics – some of which would be compulsory and others optional – which apply the standard tools of economic analysis to macroeconomic problems.

With regard to the set of compulsory macroeconomic topics, students need to learn about the **determination of unemployment** in the medium run; that is to say, abstracting from the normal rigidities which are central to understanding short-term fluctuations in the level of economic activity. This would allow students to apply the standard supply/demand tools to the labour market in a relatively straightforward way, without worrying too much about what was happening in the product market. It would thus be a natural development from the earlier developments of the core ideas of microeconomic analysis. Students should understand how to develop a competitive model of the labour market, with the demand for labour decreasing and the supply of labour increasing in relation to a rise in the real wage, and employment determined as the intersection of these two schedules. They need to realize that this model does not provide a very good description of reality as there generally seem to be plenty of unemployed people who would prefer to work at the going wage. Students need to understand the reasons why the labour market apparently does not function like a textbook competitive market – because it takes time for unemployed workers to locate firms with vacancies (frictional unemployment), because of the role of unions in forcing up wages above market clearing levels, and because firms may want to raise wages above market clearing levels in order to elicit goodwill and greater effort by their workers ('efficiency' wages).

We should emphasize that introducing the competitive model as a benchmark is in no way intended to suggest that other approaches are 'deviant' and that policy should therefore strive to make the labour market more competitive. The intention is to point out that the problems are likely to arise from market failures that may be endemic to the nature of the labour market; this should serve to heighten students' awareness of the limitations of the market mechanism. There is opportunity here for discussion of the role played by the institutional framework of the labour market. There is also opportunity for data analysis (e.g. how do unemployment rates differ over time and between countries?) and for field studies (e.g. who are the unemployed in the neighbourhood of the school, and what job opportunities are available to them?).

Students need to learn about **determination of the price level and the rate of inflation**. They need to develop the standard aggregate demand/aggregate supply apparatus. Initially, this would involve assuming completely flexible nominal wages and prices, so that the aggregate supply of goods is completely independent of the price level. Thus the analysis would focus on developing students' intuition as to why the level of the demand for (domestically-produced) goods might be inversely related to the level of domestic prices, and how that level of demand is likely to be related to monetary and fiscal policy, and to the exchange rate. Throughout it is sensible to work within an open economy framework, both because it is more realistic and because it is easier for students to see why lower prices might mean a higher demand for goods if this is associated with improved international price competitiveness. Again opportunities are available for developing students' skills at analysing historical experiences using readily available data sources (for instance, the relationship between the level of sterling in the post-war period and subsequent movements in prices and inflation). Hyperinflationary episodes from other countries in the past (or Russia today) might also provide useful case studies.

Students need to learn about **short-term fluctuations in economic activity** ('business cycles'), the role played by the slow adjustment of nominal wages and prices, and the potential for government policies to stabilize the economy. They should understand the key Keynesian idea of spillovers between markets which underlies the conventional 'multiplier' analysis. This is not always apparent in the standard treatment, which concentrates on aggregate demand and treats aggregate supply as completely elastic with the labour market pushed entirely into the background. Rather than approaching it in this fashion we think that the key economic idea of market interaction can best be represented by using the standard labour market and aggregate demand/aggregate supply diagrams together. This is illustrated in Figure 2, in which realistically the real wage is initially somewhat too high to generate full employment $(W/P)_0$. The corresponding employment level is $L_0$, which in turn corresponds to a price level $P_0$, and an output level $Y_0$. Now suppose there is a fall in demand for domestic goods; for example, because of a deterioration in investors' 'animal spirits' or a slowdown in the rest of the world. Then aggregate demand falls from $AD_0$ to $AD_1$ and if prices do not change the most firms can sell will be $Y_1$, with associated employment level $L_1$. Firms are thus constrained by a lack of demand. However, unemployment has now risen by an amount $L_0 - L_1$ and this may lead to a further reduction in aggregate demand to $AD_2$ as consumers cut back their expenditures in the face of rising unemployment. This in turn aggravates the labour market problem still further, and so on.

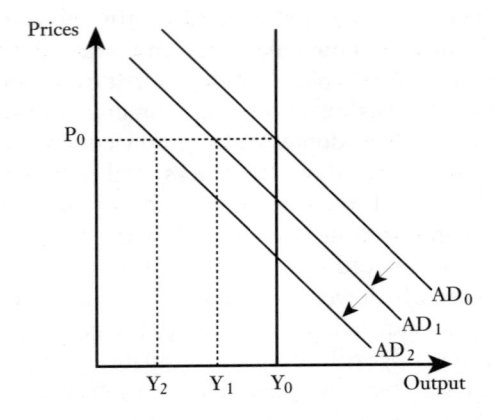

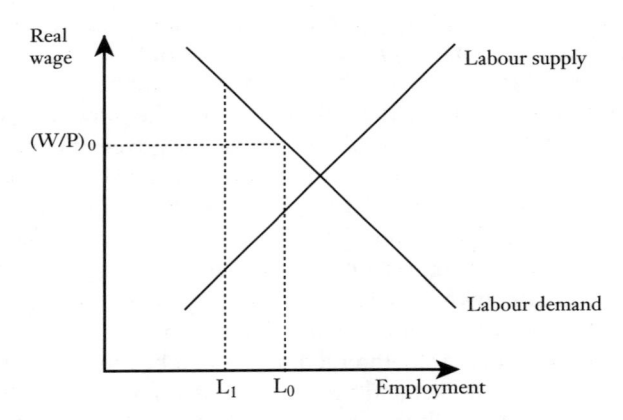

**Figure 2** The standard diagrams for the labour market and aggregate demand as a function of aggregate supply

Although this diagrammatic treatment may lack the algebraic neatness of the usual 'multiplier' analysis, we feel it does a better job in focusing attention on the key economic concepts. It can be used as a basis for discussing how wage and price adjustment could get the economy back to $Y_0$ (but not necessarily to full employment unless the market failure that led to real wages being too high in the first place was removed). It can also show how government fiscal or monetary action could substitute for this price and wage adjustment, and thus act to stabilize the economy. Study of post-war British experience offers plenty of scope for data analysis, case studies, etc.

Finally, students need to learn about **international trade**, the standard arguments about the gains from the exploitation of comparative advantage and the impact of tariffs, quotas and other trade measures. They need to consider how well this analysis explains the pattern of world trade – doing fairly well at explaining the pattern of trade between the developed and less developed countries, but less well for trade within the developed countries where there is much two-way trade in goods such as motor cars or electrical appliances.

## Economic history

*Students should have an in-depth appreciation of the factual and analytical material that is necessary to understand the macroeconomic development over time of a central facet of economic policy-making, and the microeconomic development over time of a major institution or sector of the economy. Thus, for example, the macro topic could be UK monetary and fiscal policy in the past fifteen years. The micro topic could be an economic and historical analysis of the UK car industry or trade unionism in the UK since 1950.*

There are at least four reasons why the group thought it would be desirable to include some aspects of economic history in a revised A level economics course. The first is that almost all A level students are largely ignorant of any economic developments that occurred more than three or four years before they began A level studies. It is thus essential that they should be given at least some indication of the relevant historical background because without this they will have no sense of the context in which current economic issues are discussed. They will also be unable to acquire a proper understanding of why economists hold a particular theoretical view at a particular time, or how they come to change their views (for example, in relation to the desirability and efficacy of monetary policy).

The second reason is that it is extremely important to give students an appreciation of the significance of the historical dimension, and to instil the vital sense that past experience (e.g. of technological change and employment, or competition policy and the growth of firms, or fiscal policy and stop–go cycles in investment) can strongly influence the subsequent behaviour of economic agents, whether as policy-makers or as workers, shareholders, and managers.

A third factor is the need to develop students' understanding and recognition of the importance of the institutional background. The exchange rate, for example, should be seen not simply as an abstract variable but as part of a specific international economic system which changes over time, and which thus has special institutional features and attributes in any particular period. Similarly the firm will be better appreciated if it is not seen as an unchanging abstraction but as something that evolves over time, and that might behave differently (e.g. in relation to the issue of equity capital) in different circumstances.

Finally, history provides examples which enable us to illustrate the use of particular theoretical concepts and techniques, helping to give them more meaning and intelligibility.

An attractive way to capture as many as possible of these various benefits as part of an economics course would be to adopt two separate approaches. The first would consist of a module designed to provide an overall historical and institutional background for a specific stage of the course. The second would introduce historical material either as part of any particular context or as an illustration of the principles under discussion.

We are mindful of the time demand upon economics teachers, as well as the limited attractions to many teachers and potential students of the first of these two approaches. We therefore recommend that within a major branch of both macroeconomics and microeconomics, economic history be introduced by relating the issue at hand to its development over time. In the area of macroeconomics, a 10–20 year spell of economic history appertaining to recent monetary and fiscal policy could be used as a factual and analytical base. From this students would be expected to construct thoughtful responses to questions that might be cast in a way which required the selection of factual material and economic analysis to construct an argument. For example:

> To what extent did the Conservative government's monetary strategy under Mrs Thatcher mark a clear departure from that of the preceding Labour government?
>
> To what extent is it true to say that monetary policy in the period 1979–1988 showed little economic consistency?
>
> Was macroeconomic policy under Mrs Thatcher different from that in the 1970s primarily because of its fiscal stance rather than monetary tightness?

In approaching questions of this nature, students can be given an important educational exposure to the careful construction of economic arguments and the judicious selection of appropriate material in order to make an economic case for or against a particular conjecture. These skills are not easily obtained, but economics teachers ought to encourage their students to develop in this way.

## Applied data analysis

*Development of the applied skills of young people is an essential compulsory component of an economics course which for many will be their last. We would expect this component to add confidence and skill in the selection, presentation and interpretation of various data sets – skills which are intrinsic to a large percentage of the jobs which 18 year old school leavers will occupy.*

We consider that introduction of increasingly sophisticated statistical or econometric techniques into A level empirical studies is likely to discourage many students. Students need to consolidate existing procedures and to practise using them in a common-sense way.

We would, however, encourage further development of data response activities, which are an imaginative and central part of the education offered at A level. Educational schemes which integrate data response with the more conventional sections of the course are to be welcomed.

We hope that the curriculum will increasingly facilitate knowledge of the sources of data and an appreciation of the strengths and weaknesses of those sources. Students should be able to make realistic assessments of their reliability and of the correspondence, or otherwise, of available data with the conceptual variables of economic theory.

Students need an understanding of the techniques by which 'raw' data may be manipulated to facilitate analysis. This will include the construction of distributions, the drawing of histograms, the construction of index numbers, detrending and deseasonalization, the appropriate use of rounding, etc. They must be capable of the simple application of statistical techniques, to include an appreciation of the weaknesses and strengths of various procedures, and exposure to the potential abuses of statistical information (as exemplified by the media, politicians etc.).

Students must, of course, be able to interpret statistics. This final component is likely to include refutation of the oft-heard claim that 'you can prove anything with statistics' and identification of the limits of what can be claimed legitimately. Thus correlation and causality will be seen as not synonymous, a single quarter's observation of a variable will be understood within the context of a longer series, the comparison of series, each expressed as index numbers, will be appreciated. Students will be able to temper their conclusions as necessary by language such as 'probably' and 'on the basis of this data' and will be able to set out their results and interpretations in a full and meaningful way, to include a clear statement of the assumptions upon which the analysis is based.

## The economic function of an institution

*It is important that institutions – whether legal entities, contracts or customary arrangements – and their evolution are explained rather than treated as a 'given' around which economic analysis will occur. Thus we propose that every student be exposed to an analysis of a major institution.*

Our intention is that at least one major institution would be studied in terms of economic determinants and functions within the historical context in which it has emerged. Some examples follow.

- **Money.** What is it? Why is it? How has it evolved? How is it evolving? Why are some things acceptable as money but others not?
- **Firms.** Why do they exist? How have they evolved? What is the essence of a 'firm'? What accounts for the various forms in which they are, and have been, found? Why are some transactions 'internal' to firms and some between 'firms' and other economic actors?
- **Property rights** (or entitlements). How and why have property rights evolved? What accounts for the various forms they take (private, public, common)? Why are there rights specified for some entities but not others? Is it helpful to see market analysis essentially as trades in rights to use goods in particular ways? What are the predictable consequences of different types of right? How ought they to be evaluated?
- **The family.** Why has the family evolved? What characterizes the family? What rights structures exist in different types of family? Family issues: female/male roles, number of 'husbands'/'wives', extensiveness of the family, choice of number of children, investment in children, quality of parenting, household production functions. Links with sociology/ anthropology.
- **Public authorities** of various kinds (e.g. the behaviour bureaux, regulatory/audit agencies, public sector management). Why do they take the form they do? Need they be public? How are they evaluated, monitored and/or controlled and by whom?

## OPTIONS

It is desirable that students should work in some depth within a limited range of areas. This should enable them to gain

- experience in the selection and application of core economic ideas
- an understanding of the interpretation and use of data

- a deeper understanding of government policy-making within certain areas
- a basis for formulating worthwhile project topics.

Options enable teachers to focus on areas of interest to students in a particular school or college, providing an opportunity for study in depth. Furthermore, teachers can more easily sustain their own interest in the material if provided with the opportunity of building up a portfolio of in-depth analysis – some of which might be culled from recent volumes of specialist journals – appertaining to work in a particular area. In this way teachers might become more enabled to share in recent specialist research than would otherwise be possible. Such an integration of economics graduates within the teaching profession into the ongoing research literature is surely to be encouraged if it is consistent with the teacher's professional contribution.

What characterizes an area which is suitable as an option topic? Firstly, such an area will be rich in opportunities for confirming, interpreting and operationalizing the subject core. The area of environmental economics is an excellent one to develop in this way the concept of externalities.

The option topics can provide everyday contexts within which students are required to select appropriate concepts to understand both resource allocation, and policy intervention. Thus, for example, transport problems give rise to situations where students can (i) spot the use of price discrimination and explain its form, and (ii) consider how the non-existence of markets may create mis-allocations and the need for policy.

Options can extend the core subject matter. Thus, for example, health economics creates a context in which students can begin to think about the consequences for the provision of private insurance of agents having less than full information.

Options can challenge assumptions within the core. Thus, whereas in the core we assume that markets always clear, in studies of unemployment or housing situations may arise where students will recognize that these assumptions rule out an analysis of essential facets of a problem.

Finally, options can ensure that students are introduced to a range of *stimulating* factual/statistical material that facilitates development of the empirical skills we have described above. Teaching staff need to locate analytical articles which combine interesting material with careful economics.

## CONCLUSIONS

The project's view on the new economics for 16–19 year olds is that it should be organized around the central ideas that explain the strengths and weaknesses of the market economy. This requires an understanding of how:

- competitive markets work and can, under certain assumptions, achieve the Invisible Hand theorem of efficient resource allocation
- monopolies influence resource allocation
- externalities and public goods cause inefficient resource allocation
- monopolies and externalities give rise to a case for policy
- prices in certain markets may persistently fail to clear those markets
- product and factor markets are related and adjust in the event of changing circumstances
- aggregate output and cycles in aggregate output are determined, giving rise to government stabilization policies.

# Part 2
# Teaching and learning the new economics

## INTRODUCTION

During the course of the project, the Teaching and Learning Group repeatedly asked colleagues in a variety of different contexts 'What are the characteristics of the performance of a successful student of economics?' Responses were remarkably consistent. When asked to prioritize, teachers described students as follows:

'they consider bias'
'they use evidence'
'they make reasoned judgements'
'they display an absence of mechanical principle'
'they see the wrinkles'
'they use economic ideas in argument'
'they see economic concepts in different contexts'
'they use economic theories and models to illuminate real situations and problems'
'they use appropriate terminology'
'when faced with data they select what is appropriate'
'they initiate'
'they use concepts creatively'
'they see beyond the immediate argument'
'they see limitations in economics'.

All the above quotations were drawn from transcripts of project conferences and they appeared, to us, to cover three different kinds of objectives – the encouragement of a thoughtful approach, a search for coherent and logical patterns in experience, and the development of new and creative insights and meanings.

In order to support and extend this thinking, we therefore turned to some of the outcomes of research conducted in the United States by Newmann (1990), in New Zealand by Burns, Clift and Duncan (1991) and in Sweden and elsewhere by Marton and his colleagues (Marton,

1981, for example). Newmann sought to identify the characteristics of higher order thinking in social science classes. He placed great value on the reflective nature of such classroom activity which he called 'classroom thoughtfulness'. Burns, Clift and Duncan investigated sixth-form students' understanding of the term 'understanding' to reveal two orientations, a coherence and a knowledge orientation. They showed that students displaying a coherence orientation (which could be taught) gained greater understanding than those displaying a knowledge orientation. Marton considered the implication of phenomenographic studies for teaching and learning. He argued that, if the aim is to help students to change the meanings assigned to various phenomena, teaching methods have to be thought about and developed in relation to each phenomenon to be studied.

We felt that these writers' ideas about classroom thoughtfulness, students' perceptions of understanding, and learning as changing meaning would be useful to the developing work of the 16–19 project for two reasons. They seemed to us to clarify the relationship between active, effective and rigorous learning and to provide insights into the process of interaction between teachers, learning tasks and students. We adopted the term 'economic thoughtfulness' to incorporate these ideas and as a focus for teachers' thinking. One of its useful features was that it provided an effective means of generating discussion. We also found it relatively straightforward to obtain a broad consensus among teachers about its meaning. Project members found it easy to accept that the following three illustrations, for example, showed a degree of economic thoughtfulness.

- A first-year A level student was asked to criticize the standard textbook comparison of output and price under conditions of perfect competition and monopoly, and said: 'But you are not comparing like with like ... it seems to me that the costs facing a large business are not likely to be the same as those facing a small firm'.

- Members of a year-1 BTEC Business and Finance group making a presentation on the problems faced by eastern European economies pointed out that part of the differences in economic performance might be attributed to factors that preceded communist takeover in the late 1940s, as well as to changes in recent history.

- A second-year A level student recorded at the end of an assignment: 'Before I studied Development, I more or less thought that it was their fault but now I realize that things are not as simple'.

```
┌─────────────────────────────────────────────────┐
│  ┌──────────────────────┐   ┌──────────────┐   │
│  │ THE STUDENT AS LEARNER│  │ ORGANIZATION │   │
│  └──────────────────────┘   └──────────────┘   │
│              ↘              ↙                   │
│         ┌─────────────────────────┐             │
│         │ Economic thoughtfulness │             │
│         └─────────────────────────┘             │
│                     ↑                           │
│            ┌─────────────────┐                  │
│            │  RELATIONSHIPS  │                  │
│            └─────────────────┘                  │
└─────────────────────────────────────────────────┘
```

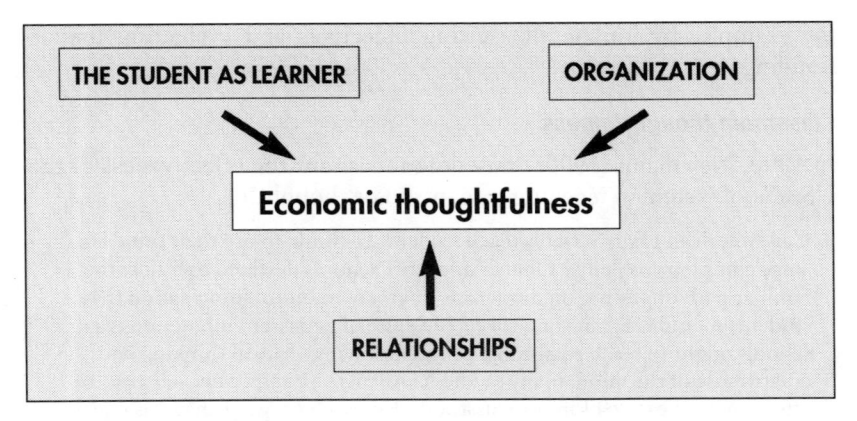

**Figure 3**  The main components of economic thoughtfulness

During a process of refinement, by means of a review of current practice in fields related to the project's work, the concept of economic thoughtfulness was further elaborated to incorporate statements about the organization of learning and relationships. As a result of our understanding of current research into learning we feel that teachers of economics need to pay particular attention to the student as learner, and focus on the development, in students, of critical self-awareness, positive dispositions to study, a range of appropriate skills and knowledge, and the ability to apply them to a range of different contexts. At the same time, teachers need to be sensitive to the organization of learning environments, and to the relationships that they develop with their students.

Figure 3 gives an overview of the main components of economic thoughtfulness. Each is considered in greater detail later (pages 43–47).

## CURRENT RESEARCH ON LEARNING

Our first task was to carry out a selective review of the research literature to determine what was being established about effective learning. We found that the weight of current research in this field places an increasing emphasis on the student's role as an agent in the learning process. It draws attention to the fact that students should be aware of the nature and purpose of what they are learning. It suggests that their implicit theories of how learning takes place may have to be challenged. It also acknowledges that teachers often take upon themselves too much responsibility for determining important processes in students' learning;

for example, by unilaterally setting objectives and evaluating understanding.

### Classroom thoughtfulness

In 1990, Newmann (1990a) raised doubts about the effectiveness of the US school system in teaching students to be thoughtful.

> Can American High Schools teach students to think, to use their minds to solve complex problems? Or are American Schools destined to follow the familiar path of passing on numerous fragmented bits of information that students memorize, but soon forget? In spite of persistent injunctions that schools ought to teach reasoning, problem solving, critical thinking and creative use of the mind, many studies confirm the conspicuous absence of attention to these goals in the classroom. Research suggests that this may be due to several obstacles: difficulties in defining higher order thinking and in evaluating student performance in thinking; class size and teaching schedules which prevent teachers from responding in detail to students' work; curriculum guidelines and testing programmes that require coverage of vast amounts of material; students' apparent preferences for highly structured work with clear 'correct' answers and teachers' conceptions of knowledge that emphasize the acquisition of information more than interpretation, analysis and evaluation.

Newmann then developed a conception of higher order thinking, which he distinguished from lower order thinking:

> Lower order thinking demands only routine, mechanistic application of previously acquired knowledge; for example, repetitive exercises such as listing information previously memorized, inserting numbers into previously learned formulae, or applying rules ... In contrast, higher order thinking challenges the student to interpret, analyse, or manipulate information, because a question to be answered or a problem to be solved cannot be resolved through the routine application of previously learned knowledge.

Newmann identified three components as necessary for students to cope with the kind of challenges generated by higher order thinking. These are in-depth knowledge, skills of analysis, interpretation and manipulation, and a disposition to thoughtfulness (which is defined as a persistent desire that claims be supported by reasons, a tendency to be reflective rather than impulsive, and intellectual curiosity and flexibility). If students are to be prepared to deal effectively with non-routine problems, teachers must organize activities which enable them to practise the skills of analysis, interpretation and manipulation of knowledge and provide the support necessary for developing dispositions of thoughtfulness.

Newmann suggested that the encouragement of higher order thinking, which he named 'classroom thoughtfulness', should be considered as a cultural characteristic of classrooms. Empirical research showed that classrooms were more likely to be thoughtful environments when teachers considered reasons and explanations carefully, when students were able to generate new and relevant ideas, and when teachers asked students to justify or to clarify their assertions in a Socratic manner. Newmann (1990b) argued that while it was necessary to separate these three elements for the purpose of presenting a framework, they should be integrated in practice. Interestingly, research findings indicated that, whereas the degree of classroom thoughtfulness varied considerably, its occurrence was independent of the age, achievement level, and ethnic make-up of classes.

While elements of Newmann's work are not directly applicable to practice in British schools and colleges, there seem to be clear parallels with our classroom experience especially in respect of failure to define thoughtfulness. How might we recognize a thoughtful classroom? What strategies are likely to be most effective in promoting such thought? Newmann's work provides a theoretical basis for the development of appropriate classroom activities.

Newmann highlights the need to consider an appropriate balance between the development of in-depth knowledge, favourable dispositions and appropriate skills. He suggests that this is crucial in generating thoughtfulness. This appears to be consistent with the feelings of many teachers of economics. It is arguable that traditional courses place far too heavy an emphasis on in-depth knowledge of the subject, thus preventing the development of necessary skills and dispositions, whilst some newer courses over-emphasize skills to the detriment of the other components. Newmann suggests that the key lies in the provision of opportunities for students to develop and test their thinking in non-routine situations. This is a view shared by SEAC (1990) in its consultation document on draft principles for A and AS levels.

> Depth and rigour involve the initiation of students into the common concepts and language which underpin disciplines. Students learn to recognize both explicitly and implicitly what constitutes grounds for argument and the tests for truth within disciplines. They also acquire awareness of the methodology of the discipline, including what constitutes evidence, and the procedures that may be used to expose new evidence, to develop new lines of argument and to criticize existing arguments and evidence. Depth and rigour arise from the learning opportunities that allow students to gain experience of disciplines by active involvement in their essential processes, for example, problem solving or active enquiry. Ultimately, students should be in a position to appraise

critically the received notions and methodology of the disciplines they have studied. However, skills and concepts should be developed in such a way that potentially they may be applied to unfamiliar contexts.

## *Students' perceptions of understanding*

The second source of influence on our thinking came from research undertaken in New Zealand by Burns, Clift and Duncan (1991) into students' and teachers' perceptions of understanding in sixth-form chemistry. This research placed particular emphasis on identifying and describing two distinct orientations in the ways that students approached their learning. Students adopting a 'coherence orientation' were concerned about the relationship between pieces of new information and between these and recalled information. They wanted to know the meanings of terms and why things happened as they did. They felt that they had achieved understanding when they could make a whole from many bits of received information together with those that they recalled from memory. They often said that they understood when everything 'clicked'. In the words of a high achieving student this meant 'knowing something from within, having it all sorted out inside, rather than knowing what to do and not knowing why; knowing why you do things rather than just following rules'.

In contrast, students with a knowledge orientation associated understanding with the recognition of terms and the memorization of facts and rules. Such students were concerned with the detail of knowing what and knowing how; for example, knowing the procedures for solving a problem or completing a task.

Burns and associates found that these two groups of students assessed their understanding differently. Those adopting a coherence orientation talked of constructing mental images ('clear pictures in my mind') which were useful and valued in talking about the topic to others, whereas 'when you partly understand you don't want to talk about it'. Students favouring a knowledge orientation placed greater reliance on marks and other feedback from teachers.

Those students who were high achievers tended to use a coherence orientation while those who did less well tended to use a knowledge orientation. Unexpectedly they also found that most students set out on their studies employing a coherence orientation but were often indirectly encouraged by their teachers to adopt a knowledge orientation. Teachers tended to focus on examination skills – short answer and multiple choice questions – and failed to use a coherence orientation which might include, for example, giving time for peer group discussion, creating a supportive environment for students to ask questions and clearly valuing the efforts made by students to achieve understanding.

We felt that Burns' work was deeply significant for the project because it pointed to the kind of activities which would encourage a coherence orientation and thereby raise levels of achievement. We felt that these would help teachers to exploit the opportunities presented at the start of A level work when students tend to display a coherence orientation. By giving time for peer group discussion, creating a supportive environment for students to ask questions and clearly valuing the efforts made by them to achieve understanding, teachers could build on their natural predisposition for coherence.

The way that economics at 16–19 is currently taught to many students delays the 'when everything clicks into place' stage to the very end of the course, if at all. It is only then that students have covered all the extensive syllabus topics and are in a position to put everything together and achieve an overall understanding of how the different sectors of an economy might interact with each other. The recommendations of the Content Group that students should recognize and develop a basic framework of economics ideas by working in a number of well-defined and recognized contexts is expected to facilitate the development of a 'coherence' orientation.

## Learning for meaning

Of direct relevance to the project and the work of our group have been the phenomenographic studies which have sought to examine the teaching and learning challenges involved in the achievement of learning for meaning. The purpose of phenomenography is to study the ways in which people relate to some phenomenon in question; either how they understand it, or learn about it, or experience it, or deal with it. The important thing is to reveal how and what people think about phenomena, or how they experience them; the phenomena in themselves are not of primary importance. Marton (1981) has pointed out that:

> We are not trying to describe things 'as they are' (nor are we discussing the question whether or not things can be described 'as they are') but we are trying to characterize how they appear to people.

The educational significance of this approach is considerable for it implies that the most important form of learning is that involved in the change between one way of relating to, thinking about or understanding a phenomenon and another way of doing so. It follows that the most important form of teaching is teaching that brings about such change.

There is considerable evidence to suggest that many traditional courses of economics fail to enable students to change the way they think about the economic phenomena which they meet in their everyday lives as well as within the economics classroom. For instance, Dahlgren (1979) showed that successful students of economics, when asked 'why is the price of a bun one Swedish krona?', failed to consider the characteristics of the market for buns. They preferred common sense notions based on adding up the cost of particular ingredients, etc. 'Flour costs such and such, yeast a bit more and then there are labour costs ... plus something for profit'. Dahlgren also showed that studying economics for a year made no difference to the explanations offered by students. Although they had been taught to manipulate demand and supply curves to the satisfaction of their teachers, faced with the price-of-a-bun question they chose to revert to the cost-of-production explanation.

The project has undertaken its own research into the ways in which students might view and explain particular economic issues and phenomena in their everyday worlds. Six Regional Development Groups carried out 'baseline' research tasks to reveal how students thought about a range of economic issues. This research produced results broadly in line with other phenomenographic work in economics. For example, when one group of students, who had been taught about inflation during their course, were asked individually about its meaning in relation to the effects of changes in the Budget, the transcripts of the interviews indicated that they viewed inflation as a political event and the cause of increases in prices rather than a measurable process.

The most significant implications of research carried out in the phenomenographic tradition for those teachers who are dissatisfied with such outcomes, and who wish to secure the quality of students' learning and assist them to change the ways in which they relate to the phenomena of the economic world, are that teachers:

- need to be precise about what is involved in 'understanding' particular economic phenomena
- need to make allowances for the existence of fundamental differences in the ways in which students see the world and its economic phenomena
- need to organize ways to present effective challenges to students' existing views.

This research also suggests that none of these objectives can be achieved by teachers in isolation from students if changing the ways students relate to the economic world is to remain as the focal point of teachers' attention. The consequence seems to us to be inescapable. Teachers, alone, have sufficient information about students and the ways in which they respond to economic phenomena to undertake the task of designing challenging learning activities. Their role as researchers within their own classrooms is thus a crucial one on which the provision of data for evaluation and adaptation will depend.

## A REVIEW OF CURRENT PRACTICE

In parallel with our research into learning we undertook a review of current practice in fields related to the project. These included the following: International Baccalauriat Economics, Cambridge Modular Business Studies, the Associated Examining Board's Wessex Business/Economics courses, the University of London Examinations and Assessment Council's Ridgeway Economics syllabus, the University of London Examinations and Assessment Council's Business and Information Studies, Global Education, TVEI initiatives, Northern Examining Association Maths, Enterprising Maths, Geography 16–19, Suffolk Science, the Nuffield Business/Economics Project and GNVQ Business. We also gave some consideration to traditional courses, especially BTEC in Business and Finance and A level economics. We believe that the weight of evidence from current practice suggests that:

- assessment instruments have a very potent effect on teaching and learning strategies, and
- students respond positively to opportunities to take responsibility for their own learning within stimulating learning environments.

We summarize our review of current practice under two main headings: assessment, and broadening the learning base.

### *Assessment*

We began our review of current practice by seeking to determine the effect of A and AS level examinations in economics on approaches to teaching and learning. This was not a difficult task since teachers freely admit that, in order to determine which approaches to teaching and learning are appropriate, they refer first to the form and structure of the examination. They also tend to agree that the present typical A level mix of essays, multiple choice and data response papers taken at the end of two years' study effectively limits the range of learning opportunities which may be created within and outside the classroom. Multiple choice testing is often singled out for criticism in that drilling, alone, can lead to higher test scores. It is harder to train students to be successful in answering data response questions and it is common to find examiners reporting that students find difficulty working in unfamiliar contexts. But it is often possible to anticipate essay questions and these can then be successfully dealt with through the memorizing of appropriate models. Indeed, many teachers feel that success at A level depends, to a large extent, on students' ability to decode the questions set and to spot the relevant bits of theory. The implications of this for classroom activity are that students need to be familiarized with the large body of theory to which reference may be made in examination questions and also well versed and drilled in examination techniques.

Each of the curriculum development projects to which we referred implicitly recognizes that one of the most direct methods of changing what happens in the classroom is to change the mode and method of assessment. It is possible to characterize the projects by their particular mix of assessment instruments and to see clear links with and support for the kind of learning which is advocated.

The Wessex Project achieves its aim of providing continuity with GCSE by using criterion referenced marking and the inclusion of coursework. Forty per cent of the total marks available for assessment are devoted to attainment on a range of research and investigative skills to match the aim of providing students with considerable responsibility for their own learning. Modular work contributes to 40 per cent of assessment and is delivered through supported self-study packs. Students are rewarded for their ability to plan, organize and evaluate their own studies. Consequently, teachers have built up experience and confidence in providing appropriate levels of support and guidance. It is not surprising to find the Wessex project's evaluators, Craig and English (1991), reporting, as an example of a general trend, the words of one student who, on completion of the course, said that she had learned:

> a range of study skills which have helped make me much more confident when it comes to study at University or fitting in at work.

Business and Information Studies, in support of its active learning philosophy, has developed a range of assessment techniques which directly involve students. All assessment is organized through coursework, and there is evidence from evaluation undertaken by Alma Harris (1993a) that students welcome the feedback that they receive. BIS's particular blend of self, peer and teacher assessment can appear to be cumbersome and some teachers find that this adds to the pressure on them when they are also expected to become managers and facilitators of learning.

The initial phase of the Advanced GNVQ in Business has also provided information in relation to the interface between assessment and classroom activity. End tests, which include multiple choice and short answer responses, are constructed to test students' understanding of underpinning knowledge. Portfolios of coursework are used to determine the final grade (merit or distinction) received by students. Harris (1993b) finds that teachers are not interpreting GNVQ in a uniform way. Some tend to allow the end tests to dominate their teaching. Other centres reward student efforts involving less than thoughtful activity – collecting brochures and describing activities for example. Many, however, concentrate on the development of investigative, analytical and evaluative skills in order to help students achieve the high grades which are determined by the quality of their coursework portfolios. This results in well-constructed assignments and effective guidance and support which, when coupled with greater access to more complex learning environments such as work experience, generate rich and diverse learning opportunities and enable students to demonstrate high levels of skills and thinking.

On the basis of this evidence, it is possible to argue that the more flexible approaches to assessment associated with the introduction of some form of coursework assessment result in a greater variety in learning opportunities than is the case with A level. We are not convinced, however, that the comparison between the worst examples of dull classrooms generated by the narrow range of assessment instruments used at A level and the best examples of interested and well-motivated students stimulated by creative and imaginative schemes of assessment is a valid one. The danger with such a comparison is that it can lead to simplistic notions such as that moving from end-on testing to continuous assessment is the only route to the development of classrooms that are more thoughtful. We feel that this may be an over-simplification and that it should be possible, by developing clearer assessment criteria and devising more imaginative external assessments involving open-ended questions and opportunities for students to report and evaluate their research investigations, to preserve some of the best practice associated with current A and AS level examining.

At the same time, we are aware that the creation of challenging learning environments would be facilitated by the existence of a broader range of assessment instruments. Moreover, if students are to be encouraged to take greater responsibility for their own learning, then formal feedback is required during courses. These are powerful arguments in favour of allowing coursework assessments to contribute to final grades. The pressures to limit the amount of coursework in A and AS level courses appear to be based on three main considerations. First, examination boards find assessment of coursework costly to implement. Secondly, quality assurance is considered to be difficult. Thirdly, there is some evidence that teachers themselves may be reluctant to take on the extra workload. Nonetheless, bearing in mind what was proposed in the SEAC consultation document on the core content and skills of A and AS economics (SEAC, 1993), namely that:

> students should be able to identify, investigate and solve economic problems. In doing so, they should be able to use primary and secondary sources and to communicate clearly and concisely the results of their investigations

and that they should also be able to:

> identify economic dimensions of problems; plan and carry out investigations into economic problems

we feel this implies an increased role for methods of assessment, such as coursework, which monitor these processes.

Whatever the outcomes of how awarding bodies finally decide to accredit courses, the development of assessment within courses will still be required, especially in the context of assessing prior learning, monitoring students' progress and identifying future learning needs. We believe that this issue is central to the nature of the relationship between student and teacher.

### *Broadening the learning base through independent investigation*

HMI, in a reference to the Wessex project which was quoted by Craig and English (1991), stated that:

> students are learning to study more independently. In the best cases ... the staff act as tutors, who provide the initial stimulus and guidance, while students take responsibility for their own learning in a way which is an admirable preparation for working life and for higher education.

In our review of current curriculum development projects we concluded that there are a number of significant features associated with the introduction of independent investigations and the subsequent transfer of responsibility for learning to students.

- Students welcome the opportunity to plan, organize, carry out and be responsible for their own study.

- Taking students out of the classroom and giving them more responsibility for their own learning involves both risks and challenges. Outcomes become less predictable and effective management of the learning environment becomes even more important.
- Greater individual responsibility motivates and encourages most students, but those who fail to meet deadlines etc. may drop out sooner than would be the case with traditional courses.
- In introducing independent investigations it is necessary to anticipate and to avoid the worst scenarios in which students produce undifferentiated volumes of work of little intellectual worth.

One of the benefits of encouraging more independent investigative work is that it can lead students to draw on a wider range of adults other than teachers. For this reason, teachers of courses such as Cambridge Modular Business Studies and the Ridgeway scheme, which require students to undertake industrial placements, report much higher levels of student motivation.

We recognize that there is considerable evidence that excessive emphasis on content can crowd out opportunities for independent investigative work. One of the most common defences used by teachers of economics against using more active forms of teaching, or permitting study in greater depth, or simply in finding time for students to reflect, review and re-target their learning, is the perceived time constraints imposed by the need to get through a syllabus.

The experience of syllabus development within Wessex confirms the seriousness of this issue. In this case the syllabus writers and the examination board suspected that acceptance of a new course would be dependent upon coverage of most of the content of existing syllabuses. Students would also be required to demonstrate their attainment against a range of new and additional assessment criteria. In consequence students following Wessex courses are required to put in more hours of study than would otherwise be the case.

The decision of SEAC to prescribe a core of no more that 50 per cent of any syllabus at A level may give the exam boards an opportunity to design and market distinctive syllabuses permitting the exploitation of a broader learning base.

It seems to us that the explicit reference to the development of a wide range of skills which is contained in the SEAC (1993) consultative document places some responsibility on teachers to provide opportunities for the development of such skills. The document refers to the need for students to develop the skills of analysis, application, data handling, and communication. It is very clear that 'students should be able to identify, investigate and solve economic problems'.

Our review of relevant practice suggests that teachers who intend to assist students to develop the required skills by creating opportunities for independent investigation are likely to pay particular attention to the exploitation of different contexts for learning and to students' perceptions of their roles. They are also likely to be aware of the opportunities which exist within the traditional classroom environment.

If students are to develop independent investigative skills, they will need to test, refine and develop their skills and competence in a range of different contexts. There is a great deal of extra work involved in setting up industrial placements, organizing residentials, developing education/business links, and working with the local community; but they all provide rich sources of additional stimulation and the challenges necessary for the development of more independent learners. There is much to be learned from the experience of teachers involved in BTEC courses and TVEI in ensuring that where wider 'vocational' links are created, they are fully exploited and effectively managed.

Our survey of current practice also points to the importance of student 'ownership' of their learning. If this is to be achieved students need to be involved in investigative work in which they work with their teachers to identify, research, report and analyse economic problems and issues.

A considerable amount of learning is still likely to take place within classrooms and these, too, should contain a breadth and range of learning resources which permit independent study, contain relevant and up-to-date data and provide access to computers and other potential aids to learning.

## RECOMMENDATIONS

We are concerned first and foremost to achieve an appropriate balance between activity and effective, rigorous learning. Economic thoughtfulness appears to provide a useful conceptual basis from which to operate. The roles of both student and tutor in the process of learning need re-examination and review, and the institutional framework within which we all work needs to be changed to accommodate learning which is more independent and rigorous. The recommendations which follow all involve positive strategies to promote economic thoughtfulness. They focus on:

- the student as learner
- the organisation of the learning environment

- relationships between teacher and student.

These are summarized in Figure 4 in the form of criteria which are designed for use in the development of teaching materials and classroom activities.

## The student as learner

We are committed to the promotion within and outside our classrooms of a critical, thoughtful approach to the economy and its phenomena. This involves focusing on what students understand and encouraging them to think about the ways they relate to such phenomena. It is not about ways of amassing exterior, de-contextualized knowledge but about helping students to construct and reconstruct their own understanding and interpretations of economic phenomena.

The evidence considered by the group has led us to the conclusion that such critical awareness is not best developed through activities which are traditionally associated with excessive reliance on didactic methods, rote learning, short-term memorization and the use of a limited range of assessment instruments, and which offer little scope for student involvement. Nor is it likely to be developed through activities which may be more active and superficially engaging but consist of little more than processes of description, information gathering and labelling. Somewhere between the extremes of another boring lesson about revealed preference and producing supermarket trolleys laden with promotional brochures lies a range of activities which are more likely to be purposeful to those seeking meaning in a world populated by economic issues.

Activities like those developed by the project's RDGs and published as *Core Economics* (EBEA, 1994) should ensure that students have opportunities to develop and use their conceptual knowledge and processes so that they may:

- develop an awareness of how and why they may hold particular views on economic issues and events
- question the assumptions made by economists and others (especially the media)
- further develop their understanding of their economic environment.

As a result students should be less inclined to accept a received view of the economic system and be more able to make informed economic choices. We feel that they need time to reflect on their own learning, and to articulate their understanding of these processes. As confidence

## 1. THE STUDENT AS LEARNER

This set focuses on the development of students' intellectual skills and has three components: critical awareness, dispositions and abilities.

### 1.1 Critical awareness

Students should be:

1.1.1 given opportunities to reflect on their learning;

1.1.2 encouraged to explore new meanings to economic phenomena;

1.1.3 challenged on the meanings they may attach to economic phenomena;

1.1.4 extended in their understanding and capacity to analyse;

1.1.5 encouraged to develop an in-depth knowledge and understanding of economics.

### 1.2 Dispositions

There should be evidence that activities:

1.2.1 actively encourage commitment to and engagement in the learning process;

1.2.2 encourage the development of positive intellectual values (e.g. valuing evidence, paying attention to the views of others and to the rules of argument);

1.2.3 stimulate students to be creative and to think in lateral and divergent ways.

### 1.3 Abilities

Students should be encouraged to develop competence in a broad range of intellectual abilities such as:

1.3.1 problem solving;

1.3.2 decision making;

1.3.2 purposeful research;

1.3.4 communication;

1.3.5 numeracy;

1.3.6 recognition of bias.

## 2. ORGANIZATIONAL CONTEXTS

This set is directed at teaching and seeks evidence that activities offer both variety and clarity and that suggestions are made in respect of the organization of the learning environment.

### 2.1 Variety

Activities should:

2.1.1 challenge students of all abilities;

2.1.2 provide experience of a variety of learning environments and contexts;

2.1.3 pay attention to work-related and practical contexts;

2.1.4 give students the opportunity to demonstrate their abilities and understanding in non-routine and unfamiliar contexts;

2.1.5 enable students to demonstrate the richness and breadth of their understanding;

**2.2 Valid and clear intentions**

2.2.1 Do statements of learning objectives make intended content outcomes explicit?

2.2.2 Do the statements make intended process outcomes explicit?

2.2.3 Are there lists of resources and sources which will help with the issue in hand?

2.2.4 Are suggestions for the organization of the learning environment included?

2.2.5 Are students encouraged to make the best use of available IT?

**3. RELATIONSHIPS**

This section is concerned with seeking evidence that activities promote thoughtful relationships between students and teachers.

**3.1 The basis of study**

3.1.1 Are students made aware of the learning processes in which they are involved?

3.1.2 Are there opportunities for the negotiation of content, methodology, assessment, and learning?

3.1.3 Are the results of lateral and creative thinking valued and assimilated even if students go beyond the intended framework?

**3.2 Prior learning**

3.2.1 Do activities reveal, record and enable teachers to make constructive use of prior learning?

**3.3 Assessment**

There should be evidence that all materials contain opportunities for students to:

3.3.1 review and record their understanding;

3.3.2 reflect and record what they have learned in terms of content and process;

3.3.4 measure and record their performance against specified criteria;

3.3.5 set and record new learning targets.

**Figure 4** Summary of teaching and learning criteria

develops they should expect their teachers to challenge the meanings which they attach to economic phenomena. Thus, a critically aware student should be able to distinguish between a personal common-sense view and the conceptions held by economists as a result of the expertise developed while practising economics in the everyday context of the economic system – hypothesizing, collecting evidence, interpreting and using judgement. Such an understanding of economics is at a higher level than that associated with the memorization and manipulation of economic models, and ensures that students complete a course of study with an awareness of the intellectual basis, power and limitations of the economist's perspective.

The development of dispositions to thoughtfulness is closely linked with the development of critical awareness. The task of the teacher is to create conditions in the classroom in which students feel confident enough to be both open and critical in their commitment to the learning process and to the development of those positive intellectual values that are conducive to higher order argument and thinking.

This kind of learning environment encourages students to be creative and to take chances in exploring new meanings. Such reflective engagement develops and is developed by the growth in student confidence. Students who are economically thoughtful are therefore also likely to develop conventional and less usual abilities and to display the full range of skills produced through their engagement in purposeful research, through recognizing, explaining, and comparing bias and through dealing effectively with various data sets. Teachers and developers of materials need to ensure that there is ample opportunity for the development, refining and testing of these abilities.

## *Organizational contexts*

We are convinced, as a result of our review of and reflection on research and current practice, that students need to develop confidence by working in a range of contexts which include those located firmly in the current issues and problems of the everyday economic world. If successful, this should also forestall the common criticism of economics that it is too remote, dry and abstract.

In particular, teachers of economics need to build on the work that has already been undertaken to include commercial and community elements within the curriculum. Industrial placements as pioneered by the Cambridge Business Studies A level course have proved to be effective in encouraging students to apply and test their developing understanding in wider contexts. Moreover, requiring students to present the outcomes of their study in a variety of different ways, including reporting to placement providers, is another example of an organizational strategy which supports the promotion of economic thoughtfulness.

Many students choose to study economics with the expectation that the complex, exciting and sometimes confusing events and issues of the economic world will be made more intelligible. For too long, however, the teaching of economics in schools has been far removed from that practised by economists working in industry and the community. Economic theory and modelling have been used as a barrier to be overcome if students are to proceed to higher education. We believe that teachers can become true gatekeepers to the discipline of economics and that they can, if they wish, provide access to the richness, depth and power of economic thinking. We also feel that the contribution that professional economists can make to this endeavour should not be ignored. As teachers, we need to be better informed about the variety of approaches and kinds of activities addressed by professional economists. We also need to be able to identify those skills which economists use. One of the achievements of the project to date has been to promote debate and discussion between economists teaching in schools, colleges and higher education and those practising what some people have apologetically described as the 'quick and dirty' economics used in industry and the community.

## *Relationships*

We believe that teachers have a clear responsibility for ensuring that students have the best possible opportunity to achieve a set of learning outcomes which will enable them to be economically thoughtful. We also believe that the means and routes by which these outcomes are reached should be open to negotiation between teacher and student. The issue of negotiation is often problematic. For some teachers it raises the spectre of open agendas and the abdication of responsibility for teaching. For others the term produces images of chaos and anarchy.

In contrast, we believe that the concept of negotiation is at the heart of a thoughtful relationship between student and teacher. Students bring with them expectations and a set of meanings established through prior learning and experience. In our view they are more likely to take an active, thoughtful role in the process of review and challenge if their responsibility for their own learning is acknowledged and they are perceived as partners in the process.

## CONCLUSIONS

It was always the concern of our group to develop a clear view of how students might be helped to be rigorous, active and thoughtful in their studies. Superficially we had an easy task. There is a broad consensus that a lot can be done to make the teaching of economics more stimulating, active, and motivating. Some teachers have experienced feelings of liberation through involvement in TVEI and industry-related initiatives, economic awareness programmes, projects based within Development Education Centres, BTEC and A level business studies. All of these clearly demonstrate the availability of a range of strategies which bring about more active participation in the learning process. Other teachers, faced with the challenges of traditional syllabuses, have succeeded in developing active and thoughtful classrooms in spite of the constraints imposed by exam boards.

However, there is no doubt in our view that, in the past, events have conspired to encourage teachers and students into the habit of concentrating exclusively on content. Many teachers have argued that it is the restrictive nature of syllabus content which has prevented them from developing ways of teaching which would bring more meaning to students' learning. This has left students with too little time to explore, investigate, review, reflect and re-define and has discouraged teachers from experimenting with the teaching and learning environment.

We therefore consider that the emphasis given to the need to develop economic thoughtfulness by the project and, indirectly, by SEAC and NCVQ, is likely to challenge the complacency of most, if not all, teachers and students of economics. If learning is to be more active, effective and of a sufficiently high quality, there is a need for change within economics classrooms as well as in syllabuses.

## REFERENCES

Burns, J., Clift, J., and Duncan, J. (1991) 'Understanding of understanding: implications for learning and teaching', *British Journal of Educational Psychology*, vol. 61, pp. 276–289.

Craig, S. and English, T. (1991) *An Evaluation of the Wessex Project*, University of Bath.

Dahlgren, L.O. (1979) *Children's Conception of Price as a Function of the Questions Asked*, Report 81, The Institute of Education, University of Göteborg.

Economics and Business Education Association (1994) *Core Economics*, Heinemann Educational.

Harris, A. (1993a) Unpubished PhD Thesis, University of Bath.
Harris, A. (1993b) *An Evaluation of the GNVQ Pilot*. Unpublished report to the National Development Group on Teaching and Learning, Economics Education 16–19 Project.
Marton, F. (1981) 'Describing conceptions of the world around us', *Instructional Science*, vol. 10, pp. 177–200.
Newmann, F. (1990a) 'Higher order thinking in teaching social studies: a rational for the assessment of classroom thoughtfulness', *Journal of Curriculum Studies*, vol. 22, pp. 41–56.
Newmann F. (1990b) 'Qualities of thoughtful social studies classes: an empirical profile', *Journal of Curriculum Studies*, vol. 22, pp. 253–275.
SEAC (1990) *Consultation on the Draft Principles for GCE AS and A Examinations*. SEAC.
SEAC (1993) *Consultation Draft, A/AS Subject Core for Economics*. SEAC.

# Appendix 1

**CRITICISMS OF ACADEMIC ECONOMICS SYLLABUSES AT A LEVEL**

While there has been a remarkable growth in candidates for A level economics during the past ten years, at the same time the subject has maintained or even increased the intellectual standing that it occupies in the sixth form curriculum. Nevertheless several broad criticisms of the course content are sometimes mentioned by teachers and have influenced the work of the Content NDG. It should perhaps be remembered that careful criticism of the development of A level economics has helped to contribute to its present high intellectual standing, and we believe that examining constructive criticism can only positively assist our further work.

• A level content is relatively mechanical, requiring only that students learn some models and be capable of reproducing them without great thought or understanding. These models are spelled out in a vacuum of history and judgement, so that (i) the links between theory and supporting evidence are never properly made, and (ii) students do not learn the skills of assembling critical evidence towards the assessment of an idea.

• The link between theory and policy, especially in the area of microeconomics, is extremely tentative. Thus policy-orientated studies and projects are poorly informed by, and structured by, theory.

• Students know too little of recent economic history to be able to apply macroeconomic and political economy ideas effectively.

• The subject is taught in a relatively fragmented fashion, topic by topic, without the students getting much of an overall sense of how markets link the agents and institutions in the system.

• The models themselves are unsuitable because either (i) they are implausible, requiring assumptions that are blatantly false, or (ii) they present a selfish individualistic approach to the economic behaviour that students might adopt as a role model.

• Given that economics comprises about one-third of formal education over two years for a broad ability range, the content should encompass a more extensive range of issues than has been traditional.

The first criticism is potentially the most fundamental and the one that concerns us the most. The fifth criticism is to us the least persuasive since modelling generally requires abstractions from reality to create tractability, and students should be clearly advised that our models aim only to describe approximately (and not to recommend) how households and institutions should behave. We have broad sympathy with the other criticisms, and the proposals reflect our attempt to enable A level content to address these points while affirming its commitment to certain ideas and principles.

# Appendix 2

**MICROECONOMICS: FURTHER COMMENTS ON A LEVEL**

A disproportionate share of the concern with A level economics education has been focused on 'microeconomics'. The view has been expressed in various contexts by numerous members of the teaching profession that much of textbook microeconomics is sterile and laden with dull geometry. Furthermore, micro theory is not readily integrated to the policy-related issues that are of interest to both students and teachers. In other words, a substantial segment of received theory is uninteresting, as a result of being inwardly focused on internal consistency and the logical exercises this offers, and too little directed to its application. A consequence of this is that many teachers now do not cover certain parts of the syllabus that others would regard as basic.

A recent survey of teachers' views carried out by William Mason and Ian Parker on behalf of this project uncovered a helpful fact which underlines this. They found that teachers draw more predominantly upon the macroeconomic parts of the course to achieve the underlying *educational* objectives that A level economics is intended to achieve.

To some members of the economics profession this is likely to be not only a source of concern but also somewhat surprising. Much that is exciting, fresh and useful in modern economics is arising within microeconomics, but it would appear – for whatever reason, good or bad – not to be percolating into A level studies. Furthermore one may wonder how far macroeconomics is being understood if students are uncomfortable with the microeconomic environment on which it is based.

A natural starting point for this review is to ask why microeconomics has fallen into relative disrepute amongst A level teachers and then to consider whether and how central microeconomic ideas can be made more accessible.

The explanation that relevant micro ideas are either harder, or appertain to less exciting problems, does not appear easy to sustain. Much of the lively work in micro policy revolves around variations on themes of externalities and market power, ideas which appear no more difficult than, say, that of the multiplier or the 'surprise' ideas to explain the transmission of cyclical fluctuations which have become widely taught, albeit with disputed empirical foundation.

If some of the basic micro ideas are not harder, are they less interesting? The widespread advent of project work at the micro-level and the recorded satisfaction of teachers with the lively work of students studying firms, hospitals, GP surgeries etc. suggest that, on the contrary, students and staff are extremely interested in a good many micro areas.

What then has gone wrong? Our impression is that microeconomics is perceived to be about three things: consumer behaviour, theory of firm behaviour, and factor rewards. These appear to be taught separately from that of understanding the economic problem of resource allocation in a market economy, which is included in a brief introductory discussion of command and market economies. Microeconomics for many comprises a sequence of what are perceived to be highly implausible models covering fragmented topics; it has no bearing on why Mr Gorbachev sought a market economy, or why the British Labour Party believes the market economy needs government intervention, or how economists formulate policy and evaluate political arguments.

To understand why micro policy analysis has not made greater inroads into A level teaching it is helpful, and probably crucial, to consider the motivation and presentation of the theory of competitive supply. This theory is at the core of the tool-kit of policy-research economists because modern welfare economics rests on the basic idea that under certain assumptions a market economy results in a Pareto-efficient outcome. Policy analysis is, in large part, a discussion of the problems of ensuring that the market economy can be patched up so that the required assumptions are satisfied. This can broadly be taken to mean that governments intervene to prompt monopolists to behave as if supply were provided competitively; to ensure externalities are corrected with tax/subsidy policy; to ensure public goods are provided; and to ensure that goods are allocated appropriately between the present and future. (Governments also intervene to reduce macroeconomic fluctuations, and – since efficient economies can, of course, be highly unequal in individual allocations – to redistribute income.)

But to understand intuitively why a competitive market economy without distortions has the efficiency property, it is necessary to be familiar with the basic ideas in theory of *competitive supply*, which in most texts comes replete with considerable geometry and three 'time periods' (short run: a number of firms and a factor fixed; medium run: number of firms fixed; long run: all variable). This is the material that is considered *especially* dull, and students certainly find it hard. Perhaps unsurprisingly, it is not well understood by students and some staff. (Even the better

A level students who go to university are often weak in this area.) The most basic ideas which underpin policy work – such as that under competition the industry supply curve is the long-run marginal cost (LMC) curve – appear to get lost in the geometry of short- and intermediate-run analysis. Presenting the dynamic aspects of competitive supply at this level may have had the particular effect of obscuring rather than illuminating what should be a (perhaps *the*) central part of a microeconomics education: a clear indication of the central properties – both strengths and weaknesses – of the market economy. This would begin with a clear description of how market clearing prices in a competitive system lead firms to employ scarce resources in such a way that for each product the marginal cost of production equals the marginal valuation placed upon the product. This develops the intuition of the Invisible Hand theorem. The students subsequently learn how a monopolist distorts this allocation of resources, and thus why policy intervention may be required. Neglect of this economy-wide political implication of micro behaviour both minimizes the motivation for microeconomic theory and critically weakens a genuine appreciation of a group of arguments by which government intervention may be justified. For this reason, understanding of a broad range of micro policy topics has necessarily been weakened, and hence potential enthusiasm undermined.

From both a concern with the basic ideas, and also from a pedagogic viewpoint, it may be best at A level to begin the theory of competitive supply with the long run (not the short run) and to establish the nature of the industry long-run supply curve in the special case of identical firms and no external economies/diseconomies. This can be done by (i) contrasting the representative firm's long-run average total cost (ATC) curve and the price; and (ii) explaining that profits will be positive (and thus entry will occur) if price is greater than ATC for some scale, whereas exit will occur if ATC is everywhere greater than price. Given identical firms, this readily gives a horizontal long run industry supply curve at a price equal to min(ATC) which is also equal to LMC. Then external economies/diseconomies could be introduced. Exceptional firms earning rents could then be introduced or possibly left for a course beyond A level. But students could clearly be shown without more than one diagram how entry and exit determine a long-run industry supply curve, together with the interpretation that its height reflects the marginal cost of producing output. Short-run analysis *might* then be added by fixing not only the number of firms but also a factor at each firm.

At present, schools differ considerably in what is taught in this area: a minority give the full short/long-run analysis in detail, but the majority select a variety of parts to discuss, with some passing it over entirely.

# Appendix 3

**ESSENTIAL INGREDIENTS OF ALTERNATIVE APPROACHES IN THE A LEVEL SYLLABUS**

Dr G. Harcourt

The principal alternative approaches in economic theory represent the views of an overlapping set of post-Keynesian, Marxist and institutional political economists. This overlap could be stressed, pointing out that the fundamental issues with which the three groups grapple are the intertwined processes of employment, distribution, accumulation and growth. This requires prior discussion of a theory of value and of price formation, and a follow-up discussion of the role of technical advances in the interrelated processes of price-setting, employment, distribution and accumulation.

I would start by introducing students to the central organizing concept of the surplus (of total output over necessaries and the – used up – means of production) and explain how different economic systems may be classified according to how the surplus is created, extracted, distributed and used. This would lead to a description of the capitalist system (or mode of production, if we still dare to use such a term), and of how a theory of value was needed in order that the surplus created in capitalism could be measured. I would explain why such a measure needs to accommodate both the effects of changes in the distribution of the surplus *at a point in time*, and the effects of changes in the level of activity and in the methods of production which help to create the surplus *over time* (Ricardo's problem).

This approach was developed by Marx into the concept of surplus labour, surplus value, and the process of exploitation in capitalism. This involved showing how ownership of the means of production, combined with superior access to finance by the capitalist class (outcomes of historical processes), allowed this class to decide the overall conditions of work of the dispossessed wage-earners who now had only their labour services to sell. I would explain why, in competitive conditions where no *one* member of either class has any economic or political power, it is nevertheless possible for the wage-earners to be organized and directed so that they provide more labour services and produce far more commodities than are needed to provide their wage goods alone. I would point out that actual conditions constituted a struggle between the two groups, the outcome of which was the creation in the sphere of production of a *potential* surplus and *potential* rate of profits to be realized in the sphere of distribution and exchange.

Whether it is so realized depends, first, upon the saving behaviour of the two classes together with the distribution of income between wages and profits; and, secondly, upon the 'animal spirits' of the business people with regard to accumulation. These two sets of forces between them determine whether sufficient aggregate demand is created (at the point where planned I = planned S) to absorb the potential surplus and actually create the potential profits available. One of the determinants of the distribution of income would be the pricing behaviour of the various sectors of the economy (so bringing in the work of students on perfect competition and imperfect competition market structures). I would stress that, period by period, employment and activity would tend to settle at the level where – given the real wage, the techniques of production and the productivity of the workforce – enough people would be employed to create their own real wages, those of the wage-earners employed in the capital goods trades, and the real wages of those who produced the consumption requirements of the capitalist class itself.

I would then sketch in how the happenings of each period would feed back into the methods of production (embodied technical progress), and into the saving and investment behaviour of the next period(s). This would give a glimpse of the emerging process of cyclical growth which characterizes modern industrialized economies. I would also include financial factors; for example, the roles of banks and stock exchanges in constituting the ultimate constraint on accumulation (and, latterly, consumption!) as well as gathering up past and present saving. I would mention the important role of retained profits in affecting the rate of investment, given the state of long-term expectations. And, to complete the story, as it were, I would cover the government with its taxing and expenditure roles (and its desire to be re-elected). and open economy factors, real *and* financial.

Finally, I would include a short section on how these alternative approaches try to start from real world observations of behaviour, trends and regularities, which are then simplified in order to make them manageable in simple models. This could be contrasted with the process of building up theory from simple axioms, sometimes based on introspection (*à la* Robbins).